D1617416

FM 17-76

WAR DEPARTMENT FIELD MANUAL

M4 SHERMAN
MEDIUM TANK
CREW MANUAL

BY WAR DEPARTMENT

DECLASSIFIED

WAR DEPARTMENT • 15 SEPTEMBER 1944

CREW DRILL AND
SERVICE OF THE PIECE
MEDIUM TANK, M4 SERIES
(105-MM HOWITZER)

W A R   D E P A R T M E N T — 1 5   S E P T E M B E R   1 9 4 4

United States Government Printing Office
Washington 1944

WAR DEPARTMENT
WASHINGTON 25, D.C. 15 September 1944

FM 17–76, Crew Drill and Service of the Piece Medium Tank, M4 Series (105-mm Howitzer), is published for the information and guidance of all concerned.

[A.G. 300.7 (15 September 1944)]

BY ORDER OF THE SECRETARY OF WAR:

G. C. MARSHALL,
Chief of Staff.

OFFICIAL:

J. A. ULIO,
Major General,
The Adjutant General.

DISTRIBUTION:

D 17 (10); R 17(5); I Bn 7 (25), 17 (30)
Interested Battalions
7   T/O & E 7-25
17   T/O & E 17-25

TABLE OF CONTENTS

CREW DRILL AND
SERVICE OF THE PIECE
MEDIUM TANK, M4 SERIES*

(105-MM HOWITZER)

Section I

GENERAL

---

1. PURPOSE AND SCOPE. This manual is designed to present instructional material for the platoon leader and tank commander in training the members of the crew of the medium tank with 105-mm howitzer for combat. It is to be used as a guide to achieve orderly, disciplined, efficient execution of mounted and dismounted action, and precision, accuracy, and speed in the service of the piece. It provides a logical and thorough routine for all inspections of the vehicle and its equipment.

2. REFERENCES. See FM 21-6, FM 21-7, and FM 21-8.

---

* For military terms not defined in this manual see FM 20-205.

Section II

CREW COMPOSITION
AND FORMATIONS

---

3. COMPOSITION. The medium tank crew is composed of five members:

Tank commander _____(LIEUTENANT or
                                SERGEANT)

Gunner _____(GUNNER)

Bow Gunner (assistant
driver (radio operator in
tanks equipped with
SCR-506)) _____(BOG)

Tank driver _____(DRIVER)

Cannoneer (loader and
assistant gunner) (tends
voice radio) _____(LOADER)

4. FORMATIONS. a. Dismounted posts. The crew forms in one rank. The tank commander takes post two yards in front of the right track, facing the front. The gunner, bow gunner, driver, and cannoneer, in order, take posts on the left of the tank commander at close interval.

b. Mounted posts. The crew forms mounted as follows:

(1) *Tank commander.* In the turret, standing on the floor, or sitting or standing on the rear turret seat.

(2) *Gunner.* On the gunner's seat, on the right of the gun.

2

(3) *Bow gunner.* In the bow gunner's seat.

(4) *Driver.* In the driver's seat.

(5) *Cannoneer.* Standing in the turret, or sitting on the cannoneer's seat at the left of the gun.

CREW

CONTROL

---

5. OPERATION OF INTERPHONE AND RADIO.

a. The crew must practice continually with the interphone to obtain its maximum value during combat. It will be used for tank control during operation of the vehicle, radio operation being interrupted during that time.

(1) Helmets and microphones should be worn at all times during crew drill. As standard operating procedure, after mounting, headsets and microphones. are tested according to the following procedure:

(a) *Cannoneer. 1.* Turns OFF-ON switch of radio receiver to ON. (See TM 11–600 for operation of radio and interphone.)

2. Turns OFF-ON switch of transmitter (SCR-508, SCR-528) to ON. (Allow 30 seconds for tubes to warm.)

3. Pushes button of the assigned channel number until it locks.

(b) *Crew members.* Each crew member inserts the plug of the short cord, extending from his earphones, into the breakaway plug of the headset extension cord of his interphone control box. The microphone is fastened securely in its proper position on the throat or lip to produce maximum clarity of transmission. The microphone is connected to the breakaway plug on the microphone cord of the control box.

(c) *Commander. 1.* The tank commander depresses the switch on his microphone cord, and orders,

4

Figure 1. Medium tank, M4 (105-mm howitzer)—front view.

CHECK INTERPHONE. (NOTE: This command is used when the crew mounts by any other method than the drills given in paragraph 8 or 24. In those drills the "Ready" report constitutes the interphone check.) Each member of the crew in the following order: gunner, bow gunner, driver, cannoneer, throws his radio-interphone switch to INT, depresses his microphone switch and reports: BOG CHECK, LOADER CHECK, etc. Upon completion of his report, he immediately returns his switch to RADIO. During this procedure, each crew member adjusts the volume control on his interphone control box to the desired level. *Care must be taken that the microphone switch does not remain in the locked position.* Likewise, the electric cords and the suspension strap must not be

5

wrapped around the hand switch lest they press down on the switch button and cause the dynamotor to burn out.

2. Upon completion of the interphone check at the end of the Before Operation Inspection, or during combat at the last opportunity before the imposition of radio silence, the tank commander tests the operation of the tank radio within the net. To do this he turns his radio-interphone switch to RADIO and either waits for the platoon net to be opened by the NCS or, if the net is open, reports that the Before Operation Inspection is complete.

(2) *Control box positions.* Interphone control box positions are as follows:

(*a*) *Driver.* On blower bracket above transmission.

Figure 2. Medium tank, M4 (105-mm howitzer)—side view.

6

(b) *Bow gunner.* On blower bracket above transmission.

(c) *Gunner.* On right wall of turret to his right.

(d) *Tank commander.* On right wall of turret next to gunner's control box. He controls his transmission by manipulating the switch on his control box, marked RADIO-INT, to the type of transmission desired.

(e) *Cannoneer.* On left wall of turret to his rear beside the radio.

(3) *Switches.* The RADIO-INT switches on all control boxes, except the tank commander's, must be set on RADIO. This is the normal position for interphone operation. The tank commander's switch will be set at INT most of the time; he will change it to RADIO only as he desires radio communication. Except in an emergency, *no one but the tank commander* may operate the RADIO-INT switch on his control box. In an emergency, a member of the tank crew may communicate with the tank commander or another crew member by throwing his control box switch to INT; but this action will interrupt the tank commander's radio reception. It is the duty of the tank commander to monitor his radio receiver at all times except when speaking over the interphone or transmitting over the radio.

b. **First echelon radio check.** As a part of the daily Before Operation Inspection the tank commander will make the following first echelon radio check:

(1) *Cords.* (a) See that insulation and plugs are dry, unbroken, clean, and making good contact.

(b) Arrange loose cordage to prevent its entangling personnel or equipment.

(2) *Antenna.* See that—

(a) Mast is complete, held securely by lock screw on mast base, and sections are tight and taped.

(*b*) Leads at transmitter, receiver, and mast base are intact, properly insulated, and tightly connected.

(*c*) Mast base is clean, tight, and not cracked.

(*d*) Insulators passing through armor plate and bulkheads are whole and in place.

(3) *Set mountings, snaps, snubbers, etc.* Check for security and condition.

(4) *Microphones, headsets, and controls.* Check for condition and proper position. Replace from spares if necessary and turn in defective items for repair or replacement.

(5) *Spare antenna sections.* See that they are correctly placed in the roll and stowed to avoid being damaged or interfering with personnel.

(6) *Ground lead.* Check connection at both ends.

(7) *Tubes.* See that spare tubes are sealed in containers bearing date of last test. Turn in defective tubes at the earliest opportunity.

(8) *Fuses.* Check condition, and spare supply for numbers and proper rating.

(9) *Cleanliness.* See that both radio and equipment are clean.

(10) *Battery voltage.* Have driver check battery voltage. If it is low, warn cannoneer to start auxiliary generator (have this started whenever radio is operated continuously and tank engine is not running).

(11) *Crystals.* Check for number, position and frequency. Be sure required crystals are present.

c. It is the duty of each man invariably to check his personal interphone equipment upon mounting the tank; he should see that it is properly maintained, and report any difficulties to the tank commander.

d. Definite tank control, commands, and terminology are set forth in paragraph 6. The desirability and necessity of adhering to this specific language cannot be overemphasized. General conversation on the interphone causes misunderstanding and disorder and is harmful to discipline.

6. INTERPHONE LANGUAGE. a. Terms.

Tank commander _____LIEUTENANT or
                             SERGEANT

Driver _____DRIVER

Gunner _____GUNNER

Cannoneer _____LOADER

Bow gunner _____BOG

Any tank _____TANK

Armored car _____ARMORED CAR

Any unarmored vehicle __TRUCK

Any antitank gun _____ANTITANK

Infantry _____DOUGHS

Machine gun _____MACHINE GUN

Airplane _____PLANE

b. Commands for movement of tank.

To move forward _____DRIVER MOVE OUT

To halt _____DRIVER STOP

To reverse _____DRIVER REVERSE

To decrease speed _____DRIVER SLOW
                             DOWN

To turn right 90° _____DRIVER CLOCK 3–
                             STEADY . . . . . ON

To turn left 60° _____DRIVER CLOCK 10–
                             STEADY . . . . . ON

To turn right (left) 180° __DRIVER CLOCK 6
                             RIGHT (LEFT)–
                             STEADY . . . . . ON

To have driver move ----DRIVER MARCH ON
 toward a terrain fea- WHITE HOUSE
 ture or reference point, (HILL, DEAD TREE,
 the tank being headed ETC.)
 in proper direction.

To follow in column -----DRIVER FOLLOW
 THAT TANK
 (DRIVER FOLLOW
 TANK NO. B-9)

To follow on road or trail _DRIVER RIGHT ON
 ROAD (DRIVER
 RIGHT ON TRAIL)

To start engine ---------DRIVER CRANK UP

To stop engine ---------DRIVER CUT
 ENGINE

To proceed in a specific --DRIVER THIRD
 gear GEAR (FIRST GEAR)
 (FOURTH GEAR)

To proceed at same speed _DRIVER STEADY

c. Commands for control of turret.

To traverse turret -------GUNNER TRAVERSE
 LEFT (RIGHT)

To stop turret traverse ----GUNNER STEADY
 . . . . . ON

d. Fire orders. See FM 17-12.

Section IV

CREW

DRILL

---

7. DISMOUNTED DRILL. a. To form crew. Being dismounted, the crew takes dismounted posts at the command FALL IN.

b. To break ranks. Crew being at dismounted posts, at the command FALL OUT, the crew breaks ranks. Crew members habitually fall out to the right of the tank.

c. To call off. Crew being at dismounted posts, at the command CALL OFF, the members of the crew call off in turn as follows:

(1) Tank commander _____"SERGEANT" (or
                                        "LIEUTENANT")
(2) Gunner _____"GUNNER"
(3) Bow gunner _____"BOG"
(4) Driver _____"DRIVER"
(5) Cannoneer _____"LOADER"

d. To change designation and duties. (1) Crew being at dismounted posts, at the command FALL OUT SERGEANT (GUNNER) (DRIVER)–

(*a*) The man designated to fall out moves by the rear to the left flank position and becomes cannoneer.

(*b*) The crew members on the left of the vacated post move smartly to the right one position and prepare to call off their new designations.

(*c*) The acting tank commander starts calling off as soon as the crew is re-formed in line.

(2) The movement may be executed by having any member of the crew fall out except the cannoneer.

(3) All movements should be executed with snap and precision and at double time.

8. TO MOUNT. Crew being at dismounted posts.

Tank Commander	Gunner	Bow Gunner	Driver	Cannoneer
Command: PRE-PARE TO MOUNT.				
About face. Command: MOUNT.	About face.	About face.	About face.	About face.
Stand fast.	Mount right fender.	Stand fast.	Stand fast.	Mount left fender.
Mount right fender.	Mount right sponson.		Mount right fender.	Mount left sponson.
Mount right sponson.	Enter turret and take post.	Mount right fender.	Enter driver's seat.	Enter turret and take post.
Enter turret and take post.		Enter bog's seat.	Close battery master switches.	Turn on radio.

12

Tank Commander	Gunner	Bow Gunner	Driver	Cannoneer
Connect breakaway plugs. Command: REPORT.	Connect breakaway plugs. Report "Gunner ready".	Connect breakaway plugs. Report "Bog ready".	Connect breakaway plugs. Report "Driver ready".	Connect breakaway plugs. Report "Loader ready".

9. TO CLOSE AND OPEN HATCHES. a. To close hatches. Crew being at mounted posts.

Tank Commander	Gunner	Bow Gunner	Driver	Cannoneer
Command: CLOSE HATCHES.	Release turret traversing lock and insure that turret weapons do not block hatches.			

Tank Commander	Gunner	Bow Gunner	Driver	Cannoneer
Close hatch. Command: REPORT.		Close hatch. Raise periscope.	Close hatch. Raise periscope.	Close hatch.
	Report "Gunner ready".	Report "Bog ready".	Report "Driver ready".	Report "Loader ready".

b. To open hatches. Crew being at mounted posts.

Tank Commander	Gunner	Bow Gunner	Driver	Cannoneer
Command: OPEN HATCHES.	Release turret traversing lock and insure that turret weapons do not block hatches.	Lower periscope.	Lower periscope.	

14

Tank Commander	Gunner	Bow Gunner	Driver	Cannoneer
Open hatch. Command: REPORT.	Report "Gunner ready".	Open hatch. Report "Bog ready".	Open hatch. Report "Driver ready".	Open hatch. Report "Loader ready".

10. TO DISMOUNT. Crew being at mounted posts, turret straight ahead.

Tank Commander	Gunner	Bow Gunner	Driver	Cannoneer
Command: PREPARE TO DISMOUNT.				
Disconnect breakaway plugs.	Disconnect breakaway plugs.	Disconnect breakaway plugs.	Disconnect breakaway plugs. Open battery master switches.	Disconnect breakaway plugs. Turn off radio.
Command: DISMOUNT.				

Tank Commander	Gunner	Bow Gunner	Driver	Cannoneer
Emerge from turret.	Stand fast.	Emerge from hatch.	Emerge from hatch.	Emerge from turret.
Move to right sponson.	Emerge from turret.	Move to right fender.	Move to left fender.	Move to left sponson.
Move to right fender.	Move to right sponson.	Take dismounted post.	Take dismounted post.	Move to left fender.
Take dismounted post.	Move to right fender.			Take dismounted post.
	Take dismounted post.			

11. TO DISMOUNT THROUGH ESCAPE HATCH.

Without weapons, crew being at mounted posts.

Tank Commander	Gunner	Bow Gunner	Driver	Cannoneer
Command: THROUGH ESCAPE HATCH, PREPARE TO DISMOUNT.				

Disconnect break-away plugs.	Disconnect breakaway plugs. Traverse turret to give access from loader's to bog's compartment.	Disconnect breakaway plugs. Open escape hatch.	Disconnect breakaway plugs. Help bog open hatch if necessary. Open battery master switches.	Disconnect breakaway plugs. Turn radio off.
Command: DIS-MOUNT. Stand fast.	Stand fast.	Dismount through escape hatch.	Stand fast.	Stand fast.
Move to left side of turret.	Move to left side of turret.	Crawl from under tank and take dismounted post.		Move into bog's compartment and dismount.
	Enter bog's compartment and dismount.		Crawl from under tank and take dismounted post.	Crawl from under tank and take dismounted post.

17

Tank Commander	Gunner	Bow Gunner	Driver	Cannoneer
Enter bog's compartment and dismount.	Crawl from under tank and take dismounted post.		Move to bog's compartment and dismount.	
Crawl from under tank and take dismounted post.			Crawl from under tank and take dismounted post.	

12. **PEP DRILL.** To vary the drill routine and to keep the interest of the crew members, unexpected periods of pep drill are introduced into the training. Pep drill is a series of precision movements executed at high speed and terminating at the position of attention either mounted or dismounted. For example, the crews being dismounted, the platoon commander may command, IN FRONT OF YOUR TANKS, FALL IN; MOUNT; DISMOUNT; FALL OUT SERGEANT; ON THE LEFT OF YOUR TANKS, FALL IN; FORWARD, MARCH; BY THE RIGHT FLANK, MARCH; TO THE REAR, MARCH; MOUNT. Preparatory commands for mounting and dismounting are normally omitted from this type of drill. Posts of all crew members are changed frequently.

Section V

SERVICE
OF THE PIECE

---

13. **GENERAL. a.** The crew of the howitzer consists of the gunner, who aims and fires the piece; the cannoneer, who loads the piece; and the tank commander, who controls and adjusts fire.

b. Training in service of the piece must stress rapidity and precision of movement and teamwork.

14. **POSITIONS OF HOWITZER CREW.** Positions of the howitzer crew are as prescribed in paragraph 4 b.

15. **OPERATION OF HOWITZER. a. To open the breech.** Grasp the breech operating handle and squeeze the latch until it is disengaged from its catch. Push the breech operating handle to the rear and right as far as it will go.

b. To load. Holding a round of ammunition with the right hand at the base of the cartridge case and the left hand at the middle of the assembled round, insert the nose of the projectile carefully into the chamber to avoid striking the fuze. Remove the left hand and with it grasp the operating handle. Clench the right fist, and thrust the round home into the chamber. As the rim of the cartridge case engages the extractor, it starts the closing motion of the breech-block. When this motion is felt, close the breech by moving the operating handle to the left and forward with the left hand. *Check to see that the latch locks the handle in the closed position.* Move the body and both arms to the left clear of the path of recoil, and signal "Ready" by tapping the gunner's left leg with the foot.

c. **To lay the piece.** Bring the target into the field of the telescope by the quickest practicable method, under guidance of the tank commander or by use of the periscope. To lay for direction traverse until the center line of the telescope is on the center of the target or until the proper sight picture is obtained. Make the final traversing motion against the greatest resistance, such as might be caused by cant in the tank. Then move the piece until the target shows at the proper range indicated by its relation to the range lines of the reticle. Adjustment is calculated so as to depress the muzzle with the final motion.

d. **To fire the piece.** Before firing, move the firing switch on the instrument panel to "ON". To fire, with the right heel depress the right hand firing switch button on the turret basket floor. If the piece fails to fire proceed as in paragraph 16. It may also be fired mechanically by depressing the firing pedal at the front edge of the basket floor.

e. **Safety precautions.** (1) Before loading each round, the piece will be inspected to see that there is no obstruction in the bore.

(2) The gunner must release the firing switch button of firing pedal after firing to avoid injury to the cannoneer.

(3) The gunner waits for the cannoneer's signal that the gun is loaded and he is clear of the recoil before operating the firing switch.

(4) After firing, during range and combat practice, the howitzer will be inspected by an officer to see

that it is unloaded before the tank is moved or personnel is allowed to move in front of it.

(5) In loading the piece, care must be taken not to strike the fuze or primer of a shell against any solid object; after loading, the cannoneer must take care to remain clear of the path of recoil.

(6) Stuck rounds will be removed from the bore only with rammer, cleaning and unloading M5, or with the rammer M1, which are made for this particular purpose. The method of removing is given in g and h below.

(7) Ammunition will be cleaned and inspected before stowing and each round will again be inspected before loading.

(8) Fuzes will not be disassembled or tampered with in any way.

(9) In case of a misfire, the firing switch is immediately opened before recocking. Do not touch breech mechanism until the firing switch has been opened.

(10) See safety requirements of AR 750-10.

f. **To unload an unfired round.** The cannoneer cups his hands close behind the breech to catch the base of the round as it emerges and to prevent it from slipping out and dropping to the floor. The gunner opens the breech *slowly.* (*Do not attempt to open the breech rapidly, or the case may become separated from the projectile.*) He then removes the round and returns it to its rack.

g. **To remove a stuck projectile.** If, in spite of care in opening the breech, the case and projectile do become separated, the projectile is fired out whenever possible; this is especially true in combat where unnecessary exposure of personnel is to be avoided. If it must be removed without firing the piece, the chamber should be filled with rags to form a cushion, the breech closed, and the shell rammed loose as described in h below and removed.

h. To unload a stuck round. When a round is stuck in the piece and it is either impossible or inadvisable to fire it out, it will be removed, except in combat, under the direct supervision of an officer. The breech being open, the cannoneer takes position to receive the round as it is pushed from the chamber, while the bow gunner or gunner dismounts and rams the round out. Using the rammer, cleaning and unloading M5, insert it in the muzzle of the gun and push it gently down the bore until it is seated on the ogive of the projectile. Exerting a steady pressure, shove the round clear so that it may be removed by the cannoneer. If the weight of several men against the staff does not suffice (*under no circumstances will the staff be used to hammer against the projectile*), apply leverage by means of a 2" x 4" piece of wood or other suitable object connected to the tank by a rope at one end, or use the rammer M1, which provides a controlled and properly cushioned blow. Keep all parts of the body as clear as possible from the muzzle or breech during the operation. If this procedure fails to remove the round, experienced ordnance personnel should be called. In combat, to avoid exposing personnel to enemy fire, the round can sometimes be pried out by using the base of an empty shell case as a lever.

16. MALFUNCTIONS. Malfunctions of the howitzer may be divided into three general classes: failure to load, failure to fire, failure to extract. Below are given the causes of the principal types of failure and the immediate action remedy to be applied.

a. Failure to load.

Failure	Cause	Immediate Action and Remedy
Round does not fully enter chamber.	Stuck round.	Remove round. Check for obstruction in chamber. Check for dirty round, and clean. Check for "bulged" (deformed) round. For removal of separated or stuck rounds see 15 g and h above.
Breech does not close.	Insufficient force in pushing round home, to clear breechblock.	Withdraw round and try again.
	Bent or undersized case rim,	Turn round so that rim engages extractors, or use new round.
	Obstruction, dirt or friction, in breech mechanism.	Remove obstruction or dirt from recess if present; otherwise remove, disassemble, clean, and lubricate breechblock.
	Worn or broken extractor.	Replace extractor.

23

b. Failure to fire.

Failure	Cause	Immediate Action and Remedy
Piece does not return to battery.	Obstruction between breech ring and rear portion of mount.	Drive out obstruction, or, if necessary and jack is available, use tank jack between breech ring and shoulder guard bracket of mount, to release obstruction.
	Excessive friction of tube in cradle bearing.	Relubricate. Take to ordnance if condition persists.
	Too much recoil oil.	Remove excess oil.
If piece is in battery:		
Action of trigger mechanism restricted.	Safety on "Safe".	Move safety to "Fire".
Blow of firing pin fails to fire round.	Defective round.	Recock piece and attempt to fire a second time.
		Remove round to determine cause of misfire. (AR 750-10.) (See paragraph 15 for removal of live rounds.)

Failure	Cause	Immediate Action and Remedy
	Weak blow on primer due to: obstruction, dirt or friction in firing mechanism.	Disassemble firing mechanism and remove obstruction or dirt, clean, relubricate, and assemble.
	Broken tip on firing pin.	Replace firing pin.
	Broken or weak firing spring.	Replace firing spring.
Firing pin fails to strike primer.	Obstruction, dirt, or friction in firing mechanism.	Disassemble, and remove obstruction, clean, lubricate.
	Weak or broken firing spring.	Replace.
	Defective firing pin.	Replace.
	Defective cocking lever.	Replace.
	Defective cocking fork.	Replace.
	Defective cocking lugs, on percussion mechanism.	Replace mechanism.
	Defective sear.	Replace.

c. Failure to extract.

Failure	Cause	Immediate Action and Remedy
Breech opens, but case is not extracted.	Broken extractor.	Pry or ram out empty case and replace extractor.
	Undersized or bent rim.	Pry or ram out.

MOUNTED ACTION

17. **TO PREPARE TO FIRE.** Crew being at dismounted posts, hatches open. The anti-aircraft gun is uncovered and half loaded as the tactical situation dictates.

Tank Commander	Gunner	Bow Gunner	Driver	Cannoneer
Command: PREPARE TO FIRE.				
Clean gunner's, loader's and sergeant's periscopes, gun telescope and cupola vision blocks.	Unlock traveling lock; elevate howitzer.	Lower seat. Release traveling lock.	Lower seat. Clean periscopes.	Inspect bore and chamber of howitzer. [1]
	Check traversing and elevating mechanisms.	Half load bow gun. Clean periscopes.	Close hatch; raise periscope.	Half load coaxial machine gun. Inspect smoke

[1] If tape muzzle cover is in place, inspection does not require its removal. If cover is unbroken no foreign material has entered the muzzle.

Tank Commander	Gunner	Bow Gunner	Driver	Cannoneer
	Check firing controls (including solenoids).	Check ammunition.		mortar; load mortar.
		Close hatch; raise periscope.		Open floor compartment.
Check vane sight.	Check periscope and sights.[2]			Check 105-mm rounds, smoke bombs, and machine gun ammunition.
Close hatch if desired.	Uncover and check elevation quadrant and azimuth indicator.			
Command: REPORT.	Report "Gunner ready".	Report "Bog ready".	Report "Driver ready".	Report "Loader ready".

[2] Periscope will be already raised since after the initial adjustment for the day it should not be lowered. Lowering the periscope may spoil the adjustment.

18. DUTIES IN FIRING.

Tank Commander	Gunner	Bow Gunner	Driver	Cannoneer
Give fire orders (FM 17–12). Turn on exhaust fan.	Fire on targets designated. Observe and sense all rounds through sights.	Fire on designated targets and on emergency targets that appear. When not firing, observe in assigned sector.	Turn on ventilating blower if not already operating.	Load type ammunition indicated in fire order (inspect each round). Signal READY each time piece is loaded by tapping gunner on left leg.
Observe and sense each round and notify gunner of changes in range or deflection.	Continue to fire as directed.		Observe in assigned sector and be prepared to move tank as ordered.	Reload all turret weapons. See that all fuzes are at DELAY unless ordered otherwise.
Control driver with interphone.				

Tank Commander	Gunner	Bow Gunner	Driver	Cannoneer
	Call MISFIRE if piece fails to fire.			In case of misfire, check that breech is closed, piece in battery; recock piece and signal READY to gunner.
	Call STOPPAGE if coaxial gun fails to fire.			Reduce stoppages in coaxial machine gun.
	Tell loader when to fire coaxial gun if solenoid fails to operate.			Fire coaxial gun by hand when directed by gunner.
Fire AA gun.				Fire AA gun.

30

Determine when mortar smoke screen should be laid and give commands to produce the desired effect.

When ordered by platoon commander, adjust indirect fire from forward position.

Indicate aiming point to gunner.

Rotate turret as directed by sergeant in adjusting smoke screen.

In indirect fire:
Lay piece for direction.
Lay piece for elevation.
Set off deflection.
Fire piece on command.
Make designated corrections in deflection

Keep mortar loaded at all times; adjust range, and fire immediately on command of sergeant.

Keep record of ammunition expended for entry in gun book by platoon leader (number of rounds each type).

31

Tank Commander	Gunner	Bow Gunner	Driver	Cannoneer
	and elevation. During lulls in normal activity observe in assigned sector.			Inform sergeant when ammunition needs to be re-stowed. During lulls in normal activity observe in assigned sector.

19. TO SECURE GUNS[1]. In battle this operation is normally followed by RE-STOW AMMUNITION.

Tank Commander	Gunner	Bow Gunner	Driver	Cannoneer
Command: (CEASE FIRING) SECURE GUNS. Open hatch. Raise and mount	Turn off firing switch.	Clear bow machine gun;	Lower periscope.	Clear coaxial machine gun.

convoy seat.	Lock howitzer in travel position.[2] Lock turret lock.[2]	engage traveling lock. Lower periscope. Open hatch (first check position of howitzer). Raise seat to convoy position.	Open hatch (first check position of howitzer). Raise seat to convoy position.	Clear howitzer; inspect bore and close breech. Clear smoke mortar. Open hatch.
Command: REPORT.	Report "Gunner ready".	Report "Bog ready".	Report "Driver ready".	Report "Loader ready".

[1] The above drill is the minimum number of operations required to put the tank in proper condition to march after it has been prepared for combat or after range practice. If time permits, additional operations and checks are performed. The gunner checks sight adjustment and covers the elevation quadrant bubble and the azimuth indicator. The tank commander may order the bores of all weapons swabbed and their muzzles taped.

[2] Normally omitted in range procedure.

33

20. TO LOAD ALL WEAPONS. The howitzer is loaded on order. This is normally the fire order, but some types of action will dictate loading prior to the appearance of a target. Machine guns are clear until the command PREPARE TO FIRE, when they are half loaded. When the fire order is given, however, or if the unit is deployed for combat, all machine guns will be fully loaded. This does not necessarily apply to the antiaircraft gun, which is uncovered and half loaded as the tactical situation dictates.

21. USE OF AMMUNITION. a. The order of withdrawing ammunition from its stowage space in the tank is based on the principle that some readily accessible rounds always will be saved for emergency use. Other crew members will pass ammunition to the cannoneer if necessary to prevent his having to use these rounds. During combat, the position of the turret will affect .the accessibility of the ammunition in various parts of the tank. In drill, however, to establish a sound method from which commanders may deviate as the need arises, the following procedure should be adhered to:

b. Ammunition is taken from its stowage space in the tank in the order: (1) Three front rows left of power tunnel; (2) racks beside bow gunner in right sponson; (3) top racks behind bow gunner. The two rear rows left of the power tunnel will be saved as a reserve for action where speed of loading is of the utmost importance. As .time permits, or on the command RE-STOW AMMUNITION, rounds are moved from the racks beside the gunner in the right sponson and from the bottom racks behind the bow gunner to those which have been emptied in firing.

c. Upon completion of re-stowing, reports are given on the number of rounds remaining. For example the bow gunner reports, "Three smoke, six HE remaining in forward racks right sponson; one-two HE remaining right of power tunnel". The gunner reports, "Rear racks right sponson empty". The cannoneer reports, "Three smoke, three HEAT, one-nine HE remaining left of power tunnel".

22. TO LOAD AMMUNITION. Ammunition for the howitzer will be crimped upon assembly and should then be loaded and stowed with great care to avoid striking the fuze end or the primer on a hard surface, burring the rotating band, or denting the case. (See TM 9–1900.) If time is available, each crimped round should be tried in the piece before stowing to see that it can be loaded. If for some reason rounds cannot be crimped, each case should be tried in the piece prior to assembly of the round. All rounds of HE will be set at FUZE DELAY at this time. Both howitzer and machine gun ammunition will be passed through the hatches as most convenient under the circumstances, a man being stationed on the forward or rear hull to relay it to those in the tank.

Section VII

DISMOUNTED ACTION

23. **TO FIGHT ON FOOT. a.** Crew being at mounted posts, hatches open. Crew members, including the tank commander, keep below hatches until completely ready to dismount and go into action and until the order DISMOUNT is given.

Tank Commander	Gunner	Bow Gunner	Driver	Cannoneer
Command: PREPARE TO FIGHT ON FOOT.				
Disconnect breakaway plugs.	Disconnect breakaway plugs.	Disconnect breakaway plugs.	Disconnect breakaway plugs.	Disconnect breakaway plugs.
Order distribution of grenades.		Pass tripod to driver.	Receive tripod from bog.	

Take hand grenades, submachine gun and 6 clips ammunition.	Procure grenades as ordered.	Install elevating mechanism on bow gun; dismount gun; install pintle.	Procure 3 boxes cal .30 ammunition.	Procure grenades as ordered.	Help driver get ammunition.
Stand fast.	Stand fast.	Pass submachine gun and 6 clips ammunition to driver.	Receive bog's submachine gun and ammunition.		Take 1 box cal .30 ammunition.
		Take spare parts roll and spare bolt assembly.			Stand fast.

Command: DISMOUNT.

Tank Commander	Gunner	Bow Gunner	Driver	Cannoneer
Dismount via right sponson and fender.	Dismount to right sponson. Receive bow gun from bog.		Pass tripod to loader.	Dismount to left sponson. Receive tripod from driver.
Receive 2 boxes cal .30 ammunition from driver.	Dismount. Mount bow gun; man gun as No. 2.	Pass bow machine gun to gunner. Dismount.	Pass 2 boxes cal .30 ammunition to sergeant.	Dismount. Set up tripod.
Cover dismounting of crew. Act as squad leader of machine gun squad.		Receive box cal .30 ammunition and submachine gun and ammunition from driver.	Pass box cal .30 ammunition and submachine gun and ammunition to bog. Move into turret; connect	Help mount bow gun; man gun as No. 1.

Man gun as
No. 3.

breakaway
plugs; main-
tain contact
with platoon
leader.

b. The dismounted crew moves to the position indicated by the tank commander or, in drill, 5 yards in front of the tank. The crew members take the posts and perform the duties of the crew of a ground-mounted machine gun as prescribed for gun drill in FM 23-55 (1944 edition).

c. In combat it is assumed that the tank will be moved to a concealed position if possible, before the crew dismounts. Otherwise the driver will move the tank to a concealed position before mounting to the turret.

24. TO MOUNT FROM DISMOUNTED ACTION.

Tank Commander	Gunner	Bow Gunner	Driver	Cannoneer
Command: OUT OF ACTION.				
Supervise taking gun out of action.	Dismount ma-chine gun.	Take mounted post (leave cal .30 ammu-	Disconnect breakaway plugs.	Help dismount machine gun.

Tank Commander	Gunner	Bow Gunner	Driver	Cannoneer
Cover other crew members with submachine gun. Pass remaining cal .30 ammunition to driver.		nition and submachine gun and ammunition in front of tank).	Resume mounted post. Receive tripod; place in bog's compartment.	Fold tripod. Pass tripod to driver.
Pass bog's submachine gun and ammunition to him.	Pass bow machine gun to bog.	Receive and mount bow gun (remove and stow ground accessories).	Receive remaining ammunition; place near loader.	Mount tank with remainder of box cal .30 ammunition.
Take mounted post.	Take mounted post.	Receive and stow submachine gun and ammunition.	Connect breakaway plugs.	Take mounted post. Stow ammunition.
Return grenades. Stow submachine gun and ammuni-	Receive and stow grenades.	Return grenades.		Receive and stow grenades.

tion. Connect breakaway plugs.	Connect breakaway plugs.	Stow spare parts roll and spare bolt assembly. Stow tripod. Connect breakaway plugs.		Connect breakaway plugs.
Command: REPORT.	Report "Gunner ready".	Report "Bog ready".	Report "Driver ready".	Report "Loader ready".

25. TO ABANDON TANK. If it becomes necessary to abandon tank, the crew proceeds as in paragraph 10 or 11 with the following changes or additions:

a. Time permitting deliberate action, the tank commander displays the flag signal DISREGARD MY MOVEMENTS, and supervises the disabling of those weapons which remain in the tank. Backplates are removed from machine guns and the firing pin and guide from the howitzer. All similar spare parts are also removed. Individual weapons and maximum possible ammunition loads are carried. The driver dismounts in order with the rest of the crew.

b. Ordinarily the tank is abandoned as a result of a direct hit either causes it to catch fire or disables it so that it becomes a vulnerable target. In such instances there may be less than five seconds in which the crew can escape without further injury. At the command ABANDON TANK, crew members throw open hatches, climb out, jump to ground and take cover at a safe distance from the tank. It is particularly important in case of fire to hold the breath until clear of the vehicle. Inhaling the fumes and smoke of the fire may injure the lungs and will at least incapacitate the individual for a time.

26. TO DESTROY TANK. When the command DESTROY TANK is given, crew members first remove what equipment is to be carried away. They then destroy the tank, weapons, ammunition, and equipment to be left, as prescribed in Section XI.

27. ACTION IN CASE OF FIRE. a. Fire in engine compartment. The first crew member to discover fire calls, ENGINE FIRE.

Tank Commander	Gunner	Bow Gunner	Driver	Cannoneer
Disconnect breakaway plugs.	Disconnect breakaway plugs.	Disconnect breakaway plugs.	Disconnect breakaway plugs.	Disconnect breakaway plugs.
Dismount to rear deck.		Take hand extinguisher.	Pull ONE fixed extinguisher	Obtain wrenches.

Receive wrenches and fire extinguisher.	Pass hand extinguisher to sergeant.		control handle; shut off engine.	Pass wrenches to sergeant.
	Dismount to rear deck.	Dismount.	Dismount.	Dismount.
Start to open top engine doors.		Go to rear of tank; unfasten rear engine doors, ready to open if needed.	Go to rear of tank and help as ordered.	Go to rear of tank and assist other crew members.
	Unfasten top engine doors. Stand by to pull exterior control handle of second fixed extinguisher if ordered.	Use hand extinguisher through rear doors if ordered.		
If fixed extinguisher has not put out fire, use hand extinguisher through top doors or order use of second fixed extinguisher.				

b. Fire in air horn. (Applicable only to tanks equipped with radial engines.) The first crew member to discover fire calls, AIR HORN FIRE.

Tank Commander	Gunner	Bow Gunner	Driver	Cannoneer
Disconnect breakaway plugs.	Disconnect breakaway plugs.	Disconnect breakaway plugs.	Disconnect breakaway plugs.	Disconnect breakaway plugs.
Take wrench and screwdriver from loader; dismount.	Take hand extinguisher. Dismount.	Take hand extinguisher; dismount.	Race engine (if cranking, continue in attempt to start).	Obtain wrench and screwdriver; pass to sergeant.
Go to rear of tank; open rear engine doors.	Remove cone from hand extinguisher nozzle.	Remove cone from hand extinguisher nozzle.	Dismount if ordered.	Dismount to rear deck.
If racing engine has not put out fire, cut small hole with screwdriver in air horn-intake tube coupling.	Go to rear of tank; stand by to use extinguisher.	Go to rear of tank.		Stand by to operate fixed extinguisher if ordered.
		Insert extinguisher nozzle in hole made by sergeant; operate extinguisher.		

c. Fire in fighting compartment. The first crew member to discover the fire calls, TURRET (or HULL) FIRE. The tank is stopped and the engine shut off. Fire extinguishers are passed to the men nearest the fire, and the crew members nearest them help in any way possible to extinguish the fire. The turret is traversed if necessary. The tank commander supervises the work and orders the crew to dismount if the fire gets beyond control.

28. ADVICE TO INSTRUCTORS. a. Disciplined and effective dismounted action requires long and arduous drill. Satisfactory results can be obtained only by painstaking repetition of each movement. The technique of mounting and dismounting of all crew members is observed in detail by the tank and platoon commanders and altered, if necessary, before habits are formed. Once each man has found the most efficient method of mounting and dismounting, he is encouraged to adhere rigidly to it.

b. Training in dismounted action is best undertaken in the field rather than in the tank park. Crews are required to dismount to fight on foot on all types of terrain, and under every variety of simulated combat conditions, with full loads of ammunition. Rough terrain complicates the problem of dismounting through the escape hatch, and develops ingenuity and physical agility not possible in tank park training.

c. Instructors must explain and demonstrate to tank crews how necessary to their safety and success in combat is a high state of training in dismounted action. They must point out that skill and practice in use of the escape hatch will pay dividends. The crew keeps the escape hatch door clean and well lubricated so that its release is immediate and positive. Frequent inspection of the mechanism is made by the tank commander to see that the locking rods are not bent.

29. GENERAL PRECAUTIONS. a. Fire prevention. (1) Smoking in or on the tank is prohibited.

(2) During fueling a crew member stands on the rear deck holding a fire extinguisher with the nozzle trained on the fuel inlet, ready to use it instantly if needed.

(3) Use of gasoline for cleaning any part of the tank is prohibited.

b. Mounting and operating tank. (1) Crew members mount and dismount by the front of the tank except during range practice.

(2) Unnecessary contact with any part of the weapons or sighting equipment will be avoided. This includes—

(*a*) Stepping on the howitzer barrel or shield, or the machine guns in mounting or dismounting.

(*b*) Supporting oneself by holding the tube, howitzer shield, or machine guns in mounting or dismounting.

(*c*) Use of the shoulder guard as a step in entering or leaving the turret.

(3) Crash helmets if available, or helmet liners are worn at all times inside the tank.

(4) In operating cross country the tank commander warns the driver and crew when the tank approaches rough terrain.

(5) Where possible the driver avoids rough or uneven ground which might cause injury to the tank or crew.

(6) In traveling with hatches open over rough ground or through woods, crew members constantly

check the engagement of the cover latching mechanism and the security of covers in the open position.

(7) The antenna is lowered to prevent contact with low branches or low-hanging wires, especially those which may carry high voltage electricity.

(8) The tank is driven in low range when being moved forward in confined spaces.

c. **Park and bivouac precautions.** (1) Sleeping underneath, behind, or in front of tanks should be prohibited.

(2) In moving a tank in park or bivouac—

(a) A guide is always employed to direct the movement.

(b) The guide's position is at least ten feet in front of the tank and to one side, clear of its path, in directing the tank either forward or back.

(c) At night the guide is especially charged with seeing that the path ahead of and behind the tank is clear of personnel, particularly those sleeping on the ground.

(d) The guide moves at a walk to avoid stumbling on uneven ground.

d. **Miscellaneous.** (1) After machine guns are cleared a cleaning rod is pushed through the barrel and chamber to insure that the chamber is empty. A T-block is then inserted into the receiver.

(2) Tank weapons, except the antiaircraft gun, are fired only when the driver's and bow gunner's hatches are closed.

(3) Care will be taken, while working about a running engine to keep fingers and hands away from fans; fan belts, drive shafts, and other moving parts.

(4) 105-mm ammunition will be securely stowed.

(5) Ammunition will not be carried on the rear deck.

(6) No items of equipment will be carried on the rear deck in such a manner as to block the air inlet grilles.

(7) There is danger of monoxide poisoning for the crew of a towed tank when the medium tank or a tank recovery vehicle mounted on tank chassis is used as the towing vehicle. This danger is greatest when the towing vehicle is powered with a radial engine, and when a short hitch, such as that obtained with the towing bar, is used. Men should be kept out of the towed tank wherever possible; but where this is not possible, frequent periodic check of the occupants of the towed vehicle should be made.

EVACUATION OF WOUNDED
FROM TANKS

30. GENERAL. Wounded members of the tank crew will normally be removed from disabled tanks by their fellow crew members. The operation requires the utmost speed to save the lives of those who are unhurt as well as of the casualty. A tank set afire by an enemy hit can trap its crew in a matter of seconds; and an enemy who has determined the range and disabled a tank with a direct hit will probably continue shooting until the vehicle burns. It is essential, therefore, that all crew members become extremely proficient in the quickest methods of removing one another from the tank. Speed is the primary requisite; care in handling will be stressed only where it has been possible to move the tank to cover. If the action has ceased momentarily, or the tank has been able to disengage itself without hindering the accomplishment of the mission, the casualty is removed on the spot and then carried to a protected place where emergency first aid is administered. Otherwise the action will be continued until such an opportunity is presented.

31. METHODS EMPLOYED. The methods of evacuation described herewith are based on a two-man team, which is the largest number than can effectively work around a single hatch opening. In some cases a third man will be able to give considerable help from inside by placing belts around the wounded man or by moving him to a position where he can be grasped from above. Speed will usually dictate that the casualty be grasped by portions of his clothing or by the arms for removal. If an arm is broken, however, or if there are other injuries which will be aggravated by such procedures and if time allows, some form of sling may be improvised which will relieve the part from further injury. Only equipment which is immediately available, like pistol belts, web belts, or field bag straps, will be used for this purpose. Suggested uses of some of these items, as well as more elaborate techniques of evacuation, will be found in FM 17–80.

32. DRILL. This paragraph suggests two drills which may be used as models for evacuating crew members from any position. The composition of the evacuating team should be changed frequently to provide practice for all members of the crew in meeting various emergencies.

a. The first member of the crew to discover that another is hit and so badly wounded as to require his removal calls, BOG (LOADER) (SERGEANT) WOUNDED. If the tank is not then actively engaged and the tank commander decides that evacuation is necessary, he commands, EVACUATE BOG. The other crew members dismount, unless one man is needed to help from inside; and the two nearest the hatch above the wounded man go to that hatch to act as the evacuation crew. If the man nearest the casualty in the tank sees that his help is needed, he stays inside and immediately starts to arrange a sling or take whatever other steps will speed the operation. One of the crew takes the first aid kit with him in dismounting, or it is removed at the first opportunity thereafter. The remaining crew member, if available, helps in lowering the casualty to the ground. Before leaving the wounded man, whose position is marked so that he will not be run over, the tank commander reports by radio that he has lost one or more men and gives the location where they may be found.

b. To evacuate Bog (Driver). Tank commander commands, EVACUATE BOG. Driver or gunner unlocks bow gunner's hatch from inside; No. 2 opens hatch from outside.

No. 1	No. 2
Kneel on inner edge of hatch.	Take position to the outside rear of hatch.
Reach into hatch and grasp hands of casualty, straightening him in seat if necessary.	
Cross arms over chest.	Grasp nearest hand when arms are crossed.
Raise and rotate casualty so that he faces outward.	Raise casualty and help rotate him outward.
Seat casualty on front rim of hatch; support in this position while No. 2 dismounts.	Help seat casualty; dismount to ground in front of Bog's hatch.
Lower trunk into arms of No. 2.	Receive and support trunk of wounded man, holding it beneath arms around chest.
Lift legs out of hatch as No. 2 lowers body along slope plate.	Lower body along slope plate and support until No. 1 can reach ground and assist.
Dismount. Place casualty in carry position.	Place casualty in carry position.
Carry casualty to protected area.	Help No. 1 carry to protected area.

c. **To evacuate cannoneer**[1]. Tank commander commands, EVACUATE LOADER. He dismounts to rear deck to act as No. 1. Gunner stays in the turret to act as No. 2. If time permits he traverses the turret until the hatch is near the center of the rear deck.

No. 1	No. 2
Take position on rear deck behind turret hatch.	Raise casualty as high as possible in hatch opening, holding around chest.
Grasp casualty by hands.	
Raise casualty through hatch and seat on rear edge.	Help No. 1 raise casualty by lifting from below.
Hold casualty while No. 2 dismounts to rear deck.	Dismount to rear deck.
Pick casualty up in arms; carry to rear and lay along back edge of deck.	Help No. 1 pick up casualty and carry to rear of tank; dismount.
Help No. 2 lift trunk of casualty off tank; dismount.	Lift upper part of body off tank and support until No. 1 arrives to help.
Lift hips and legs off tank.	
Carry casualty to protected area.	Help carry casualty to protected area.

[1] Drill applicable in this form only where the casualty can be lifted by his arms, especially in the case of a big man whose shoulders are too wide for the hatch opening when his arms are lowered. In such cases the cannoneer is evacuated through the cupola hatch.

Section IX

INSPECTIONS
AND MAINTENANCE

---

33. GENERAL. a. The tank commander is responsible for seeing that all inspections are made. He receives reports from the various crew members relative to their individual inspections, and he indicates in the trip ticket or other inspection report anything requiring the services of maintenance personnel. In supervising first echelon maintenance he uses his discretion in delegating additional responsibilities to the crew members.

b. Inspection covers all personal equipment and weapons, vehicle equipment and weapons, and mechanical features of the vehicle. In combat it includes a check of the application of protective cream by the entire crew. Checks of instruments, lights, siren, track, suspension system, and engine performance are made in accordance with provisions of the appropriate technical manual; the driver fills in the section of the trip ticket covering the mechanical condition and equipment of the vehicle and indicates required maintenance work. The trip ticket should be carefully and thoroughly prepared. Any irregularity noted and entered on it, which is not repaired before the tank is used again, should be re-entered continually until it has been properly taken care of.

34. BEFORE OPERATION INSPECTION, M4, M4A1. Tank locked and covered by tarpaulin. (NOTE: For training purposes, the inspection is divided into three phases, each phase being completed before the next is begun. Crew members coordinate their respective operations to make the best use of the time available. They procure tools as needed, report and correct deficiencies as found. The turret is traversed as necessary to facilitate the various checks.)

PHASE A

Tank Commander	Gunner	Bow Gunner	Driver	Cannoneer
Command: FALL IN; PREPARE FOR INSPECTION.				
Inspect crew. Command: PERFORM BEFORE OPERATION INSPECTION.	Stand inspection.	Stand inspection.	Stand inspection.	Stand inspection.
Begin trip ticket; fill out during inspection.	Help remove tarpaulin.	Inspect ground beneath tank for fuel or oil leaks.	Remove and fold tarpaulin (4′ x 6′).	Help remove and fold tarpaulin.

Inspect tracks and tank suspension. (Visual check adequate for daily inspection of wedge nuts or lock pins.)

Supervise inspection made by other crew members.

Mount left sponson; unlock driver's hatch; enter tank.

Unlock bog's hatch; clear bow gun.

Move to turret. Unlock hatches. Elevate howitzer; traverse turret left to expose hand tools and clear air inlet cover.

Mount to rear deck via right fender and sponson.

Check fuel level including auxiliary generator tank.

Open cupola hatch.

Check engine oil level.[1]

Raise air inlet cover.

Lay tarpaulin to right of tank.

Check outside equipment.

Release howitzer traveling bracket.

[1] May be checked by cannoneer in turret compartment on some earlier models.

Tank Commander	Gunner	Bow Gunner	Driver	Cannoneer
	Pass tools to driver. Remove breech covers; clear turret weapons. Receive muzzle covers. Stow muzzle and breech covers.	Check clutch clearance. Close cover.	Receive hand tools; lay out on tarpaulin and check.	Open rear engine doors to permit ventilation. Check engine compartment for leaks. Remove muzzle covers; pass to gunner.
Command: REPORT.	Report "Gunner ready".	Report "Bog ready".	Report "Driver ready".	Report "Loader ready".

PHASE B

Tank Commander	Gunner	Bow Gunner	Driver	Cannoneer
Command: PER-FORM PHASE B.	Traverse turret manually one revolution to the left[1]; check azimuth indicator.	Open top engine door. Check the following: Oil tank breather.	Take mounted post. Close battery master switches.	Open hatch; take mounted post. Check pistol port.
Mount to rear deck; help bog open door.				
	Make sight adjustment.	Crankcase breather.	Check the following: Steering levers.	Check the following: Cal .50 ammunition.
Assist gunner in sight adjustment.	Pass cleaning rods to sergeant.	Engine accessories for security and adjustment.	Gear shift lever (place in neutral).	Spare engine and recoil oil.
Receive cleaning rods; swab bores of piece and both machine guns.	Check elevating mechanism.		Parking brake.	Shell crimper.

[1] Traverse is made piecemeal and may even be reversed for short distances to coordinate with and facilitate other operations and checks.

Tank Commander	Gunner	Bow Gunner	Driver	Cannoneer
			Clutch free travel.	Decontaminating apparatus.
				Canvas bucket.
				Hull drain valve beneath turret.
	Check firing controls.	Dismount.	Transmission oil level.	Water containers.
	Receive and stow cleaning rods.	Check hull drain valve in engine compartment.	Hull drain valve.	12 rounds ammunition in right sponson.
Return cleaning rods to gunner.		Watch operation of fuel cut-off.	Priming pump operation.	Spare antenna.
Apply tape muzzle covers.[2]		Listen for booster buzz and and operation of auxiliary fuel pump.	Fuel cut-off operation.	Auxiliary generator: opera-
Check all hatch covers.		Check air cleaners.	Booster coil operation.	

Turn engine over (50 turns with hand crank).	Auxiliary fuel pump operation.	tion, tools, spare parts (allow to run in cold weather prior to starting engine).
	Instruments.	
	Siren.	
	Compass.	Open fuel valves.
Help driver check lights.	Service and blackout lights.	Check: Engine oil level.[3] Oil dilution valve and tank for leaks.[4]

[2] In bivouac and on non-tactical marches commanders will decide whether permanent type muzzle covers will be employed for convenience or greater protection.

[3] May be checked by cannoneer on some earlier models; on later models checked by bow gunner from the rear deck.

[4] Later model tanks have no oil dilution valve or fuel filter cleaner.

Tank Commander	Gunner	Bow Gunner	Driver	Cannoneer
				Push in and pull out fuel filter cleaning control handle 10 times.[4]
				Check:
				Battery.
				Fixed fire extinguishers and controls.
				Rations and cooking stove.
Command: REPORT.	Report "Gunner ready".	Report "Bog ready".	Report "Driver ready".	Report "Loader ready".

[4] Later model tanks have no oil dilution valve or fuel filter cleaner.

60

PHASE C[1]

Tank Commander	Gunner	Bow Gunner	Driver	Cannoneer
Command: PERFORM PHASE C.				
Move to engine compartment. Check automatic oil filter.	Check the following: Gun tools, spare parts. Hand fire extinguisher. Hand grenades. SMG, ammunition, and personal equipment.	Tighten exposed sprocket ring cap screws. Observe condition of exhaust. Check engine for leaks, vibrating accessories, or parts.	Start engine (operate at 800 rpm). During warm-up check: Instruments. Engine for smoothness of operation, unusual noises.	Check machine gun tools and spare parts. Mount AA gun; check gun and mount (adjust headspace). Help sergeant close door.
Close top engine door. Dismount.				

[1] The flame thrower, on tanks so equipped, is checked in this phase. The crew member using the weapon checks its condition, mechanism, and the fuel level in the tank in accordance with the appropriate published guide. It is mounted for use on order of the tank commander.

Tank Commander	Gunner	Bow Gunner	Driver	Cannoneer
Direct driver to move tank forward two tank lengths.	Periscope, spare, and spare heads (including knob settings). Gunner's quadrant and case. Elevation quadrant. Telescope and mount.	Close rear engine doors.	Magnetos. Check hood for driver's hatch.	Check the following: Coaxial gun and mount (adust headspace). Smoke mortar and bombs. Cal .30. ammunition. 105-mm ammunition left of power tunnel. Flare launcher and flares.
Walk ahead of tank; check condition of right track shoes and inside wedge nuts or lock pins and connectors.		Walk behind tank; check condition of left track shoes and inside wedge nuts or lock pins and connectors.	Drive tank forward at slow speed two tank lengths.	
Check outer wedge nuts or lock pins and connectors; watch action and		Direct driver to move to rear; tighten inside cap screws	Drive tank to rear as directed by bog.	

condition of support rollers, shoes, and tank suspension as tank moves to rear.

Check howitzer and mount.

as exposed.

Check the following:
Lubrication guide.
Submachine gun, ammunition, and personal equipment.
Periscopes, spare and spare heads.
Ventilating blower.

Submachine gun, ammunition, and personal equipment.
Periscope, spare, and spare heads.
Turret exhaust fan.

Clean chamber and breech mechanism.

Place tools in bag.

Check recoil oil. Receive and stow tools.

Pass tools to gunner.

Help bog fold and stow tarpaulin.

Lock howitzer and turret in traveling position.

Fold and stow tarpaulin.
Open hatch.
Take mounted post.

Connect breakaway plugs.

Connect breakaway plugs.

Take mounted post.

Connect break away plugs.

Check the following:
Submachine gun, ammunition, and person-

Connect break away plugs.

Check the following:
Gun book, manuals and acci-

Connect break away plugs.

Connect breakaway plugs.

Tank Commander	Gunner	Bow Gunner	Driver	Cannoneer
al equipment.		dent form.		
Periscope, spare, spare heads, and periscope holder.		Bow gun, mount, and ammunition (adust head-space).		
Spare vision blocks.		Cal .30 ammunition.		
Flag set.		Submachine gun, ammunition, and personal equipment.		
Binoculars.		105-mm rounds behind seat and in right sponson.		
Mount antenna.				
Make 1st echelon radio check (paragraph 5 b).				
Complete trip ticket.				
Connect breakaway plugs.				

Check:
Escape hatch.
Periscopes,
spare, and
spare
heads.
Tripod
mount.
Hull drain
valve.
Hand fire ex-
tinguisher.
Connect
break-
away plugs.

Report "Gunner
ready".

Report "Bog
ready".

Report "Driver
ready".

Report "Loader
ready".

Command:
REPORT
(interphone
check).

Report READY to
Platoon Leader.

65

35. DURING OPERATION INSPECTION, M4, M4A1. This is a continuous process for all crew members.

Tank Commander	Gunner	Bow Gunner	Driver	Cannoneer
Remain alert to unusual noises or conditions.	Check operation of elevation and traversing mechanisms.	Watch instruments. Listen for unusual noises.	Check all instruments carefully. Check controls.	Check stowage of equipment in turret.
Check radio and interphone system. Check security of: Radio antenna. Outside fixtures and equipment.	Check security of: Turret lock. Howitzer.	Check security of bow gun.	Listen for unusual noises.	Check security of: Coaxial gun. Radio. AA gun.

36. HALT INSPECTION, M4, M4A1. The length of halt determines how much of the following inspection will be completed and the normal priority of operations. The tank commander will be informed of the length of halt and will indicate how much time is to be allotted to inspection and how much for relief of the crew members. (During the inspection, the turret is traversed as necessary to facilitate those *operations requiring it.*)

Tank Commander	Gunner	Bow Gunner	Driver	Cannoneer
Command: PERFORM HALT INSPECTION.				
Disconnect breakaway plugs.	Disconnect breakaway plugs.	Disconnect breakaway plugs.	Disconnect breakaway plugs.	Disconnect breakaway plugs.
Check radio for security.	Release turret lock.	Dismount. Check final drives for leaks or excessive temperature.	Idle engine (run 4-5 minutes before stopping).	Turn on radio speaker.
Emerge from turret.	Elevate howitzer; check traverse.	Check under tank for fuel or oil leaks.	Check instruments.	Man AA gun.
Clean vision blocks, all turret periscopes and telescope.	Check sight adjustment.		Check driver's and bog's compartment for oil leaks.	
	Check auxiliary generator operation.			

Tank Commander	Gunner	Bow Gunner	Driver	Cannoneer
Inspect tracks and tank suspension. Supervise halt inspection.	Check coaxial gun and mount. Check smoke mortar. Check engine oil level.[1] Check firing controls. Check howitzer and mount. Place howitzer in traveling position. Lock turret lock.	Check towing shackles. Help driver check lights. Close engine doors. Check air cleaners.	Dismount; go to rear of tank. Open engine doors. Check engine operation. Inspect engine compartment. Take mounted post. Stop engine (use fuel cut-off). Check service and blackout lights. Check the following: Steering levers.	

Check stowage of equipment in turret.

Mount to rear deck.

Check the following:
Engine oil level.
Fuel level in all tanks.
Outside equipment.

Gear shift lever.
Parking brake.
Clutch free travel.
Transmission oil level and temperature.

Clean periscopes.

Connect breakaway plugs.

Resume mounted post.

Turn off speaker.

Take mounted post.

Clean periscopes.

Take mounted post.

Connect breakaway plugs.

[1] Engine oil level checked in turret on earlier models, from rear deck on later model tanks.

Tank Commander	Gunner	Bow Gunner	Driver	Cannoneer
		Connect break-away plugs.		Connect break-away plugs.
Command: REPORT.	Report "Gunner ready".	Report "Bog ready".	Report "Driver ready".	Report "Loader ready".

37. AFTER OPERATION MAINTENANCE, M4 and M4A1. a. After operation the tank is immediately given whatever servicing and maintenance is needed to prepare it in every way for further sustained action. This servicing covers all the points listed in the Before Operation Inspection and covers them in the same order, with obvious modifications. (For example, the tank is locked at the end of the inspection instead of being unlocked at the beginning; the check for leaks under the tank is more effective after it has stood for awhile; battery switches are turned off rather than on and only after all checks requiring use of battery power; equipment is covered and stowed rather than being uncovered and made ready for use.)

b. The tank will be completely cleaned, serviced, and replenished (fuel, oil (all types), grease, ammunition (all types), first aid kit, water, and rations). *All special precautions against fire will be observed while refueling.* Crew members will perform the following additional operations not covered in the. Before Operation Inspection.

Tank Commander	Gunner	Bow Gunner	Driver	Cannoneer
Command: PERFORM AFTER OPERATION MAINTENANCE.	Clean all weapons.		Idle engine 4-5 minutes before stopping. Clean tank suspension and outside of tank.	Help gunner clean weapons.
Complete trip ticket; forward to platoon leader, together with report of any necessary 2d echelon maintenance, fuel, lubricants, ammunition and rations required.		Help driver clean tank. Help gunner clean weapons.	Help gunner clean weapons.	

38. PERIODIC ADDITIONAL SERVICES, M4 and M4A1. Services performed weekly in garrison; in combat and on maneuvers they are performed after each field operation.

Tank Commander	Gunner	Bow Gunner	Driver	Cannoneer
Command: FALL IN; PREPARE FOR INSPECTION.				
Inspect crew.	Stand inspection.	Stand inspection.	Stand inspection.	Stand inspection.
Command: PERFORM PERIODIC INSPECTION.				
Supervise inspection.	Clean turret.	Mount to rear deck; help driver clean engine and engine compartment.	Open engine doors and clean engine and engine compartment.	Mount to turret.
	Clean and touch up any rust spots in turret.		Take mounted post.	Clean batteries and case.
				Test batteries with hydrometer.

Bring cells to proper water level.

Operate auxiliary generator to charge batteries.

Dismount.

Clean driver's compartment and left interior of hull.

Operate and check.hull drain valve.

Drive tank forward as required for tightening

Help gunner tighten wedge nuts or lock pins

Operate and check hull drain valve in engine compartment.

Take mounted post.

Clean bog's compartment and right interior of hull.

Operate and check hull drain valve.

Dismount.

Tighten all wedge nuts or lock pins

Tank Commander	Gunner	Bow Gunner	Driver	Cannoneer
	and inspect track. Help perform 250-mile lubrication.	Help perform 250-mile lubrication.	wedge nuts or lock pins. Perform 250-mile lubrication, referring to appropriate lubrication order. Close engine doors.	and inspect track. Help perform 250-mile lubrication.
		Take mounted post; clean and touch up rust spots in bog's compartment.	Take mounted post; clean and touch up rust spots in driver's compartment.	
Command: REPORT.	Report "Gunner ready".	Report "Bog ready".	Report "Driver ready".	Report "Loader ready".

39. BEFORE OPERATION INSPECTION, M4A3. Tank locked and covered by tarpaulin. (NOTE: For training purposes, the inspection is divided into three phases, each phase being completed before the next is begun. Crew members coordinate their respective operations to make the best use of the time available. They procure tools as needed, report and correct deficiencies as found. The turret is traversed as necessary to facilitate the various checks.)

PHASE A

Tank Commander	Gunner	Bow Gunner	Driver	Cannoneer
Command: FALL IN; PREPARE FOR INSPECTION.				
Inspect crew.	Stand inspection.	Stand inspection.	Stand inspection.	Stand inspection.
Command: PERFORM BEFORE OPERATION INSPECTION.				
Begin trip ticket; fill out during inspection.	Help remove tarpaulin.	Inspect ground beneath tank for fuel, oil,	Remove and fold tarpaulin (4' x 6').	Help remove and fold tarpaulin.

Tank Commander	Gunner	Bow Gunner	Driver	Cannoneer
		or water leaks.		Check outside equipment.
Inspect tracks and tank suspension. (Visual check adequate for daily inspection of wedge nuts or lock pin.)	Mount left sponson; unlock driver's hatch; enter tank.	Mount to rear deck via right fender and sponson.	Lay tarpaulin to right of tank.	
	Unlock bog's hatch; clear bow gun.	Check engine coolant level.		
	Move to turret.			
Supervise inspection made by other crew members.	Unlock hatches. Elevate howitzer; traverse turret left to expose tools.	Open cupola hatch.		Release howitzer traveling bracket.
		Check fuel level, including auxiliary generator tank.		

Gunner	Bog	Driver	Loader
Pass hand tools to driver.		Receive tools; lay out on tarpaulin and check.	Open rear engine door to permit ventilation.
Remove breech covers; clear turret weapons.			Check engine compartment for leaks.
Receive muzzle covers.			Remove and pass muzzle covers to gunner.
Stow muzzle and breech covers.			
Report "Gunner ready".	Report "Bog ready".	Report "Driver ready".	Report "Loader ready".

Command: REPORT.

PHASE B

Tank Commander	Gunner	Bow Gunner	Driver	Cannoneer
Command: PERFORM PHASE B.	Traverse turret manually one revolution to the left[1]; check azimuth indicator.	Open top engine door. Check the following:	Take mounted post.	Open hatch; take mounted post.
Mount to rear deck; help bog open door.		Crankcase breather.	Close battery master switches.	Check pistol port.
	Make sight adjustment.	Engine oil level.[2]	Check the following:	Check the following:
Assist gunner in sight adjustment.	Pass cleaning rods to sergeant.	Fan belts.	Steering levers.	Cal .50 ammunition.
Receive cleaning rods; swab bores of piece and both machine guns.	Check elevating mechanism.	Engine compartment for fuel, oil or water leaks.	Gear shift lever (place in neutral).	Spare engine and recoil oil.
			Parking brake.	Shell crimper.
				Decontaminating apparatus.

			Canvas bucket.
Check firing controls.	Engine accessories for security and adjustment.	Clutch free travel. Transmission oil level. Hull drain valve.	Hull drain valve beneath turret.
Help loader check air cleaners.			Air cleaners. Water containers.
Receive and stow cleaning rods.	Listen for operation of fuel cut-off.	Priming pump operation.	12 rounds ammunition in right sponson.
Return cleaning rods to gunner. Apply tape muzzle covers.[3]	Drain fuel filter.	Fuel cut-off operation.	

[1] Traverse is made piecemeal and may even be reversed for short distances to coordinate with and facilitate other operations and checks.

[2] Engine oil level checked through rear door on earlier model engines, through top door on later models.

[3] In bivouac and on non-tactical marches commanders will decide whether permanent type muzzle covers will be employed for convenience or greater protection.

Tank Commander	Gunner	Bow Gunner	Driver	Cannoneer
Check all hatch covers. Dismount.		Dismount. Check engine oil level.[2] Check hull drain valve in engine compartment. Help driver check lights.	Instruments. Siren. Compass. Service and blackout lights.	Spare antenna. Auxiliary generator: Operation, tools, spare parts (allow to run in cold weather prior to starting engine). Open fuel valves. Check: Battery. Fixed fire extinguish-

ers and
controls.
Rations and
cooking
stove.

Report "Loader
ready".

Report "Driver
ready".

Report "Bog
ready".

Report "Gunner
ready".

Command:
REPORT.

² Engine oil level checked through rear door on earlier model engines, through top door on later models.

81

PHASE C[1]

Tank Commander	Gunner	Bow Gunner	Driver	Cannoneer
Command: PERFORM PHASE C. Move to engine compartment. Check automatic oil filter. Observe condition of exhaust.	Check the following: Gun tools and spare parts. Hand fire extinguisher. Hand grenades. Submachine gun, ammunition, and personal equipment.	Tighten exposed sprocket ring cap screws.	Start engine (operate at idle speed until temperature reaches 100° F). During warm-up check: Instruments. Engine for smoothness of operation and unusual noises. Magnetos.	Check machine gun tools and spare parts. Mount AA gun; check gun and mount (adjust headspace). Check the following: Coaxial gun and mount (adjust headspace). Smoke mortar and bombs.
Direct driver to move tank forward two tank lengths.		Close rear engine door.		

Walk ahead of tank; check condition of right track shoes and inside wedge nuts or lock pins and connectors.

Check outer wedge nuts or lock pins and connectors; watch action and condition of support rollers, shoes, and tank suspension as tank moves to rear.

Periscope, spare, and spare heads (including knob settings).
Gunner's quadrant and case.
Elevation quadrant.
Telescope and mount.
Check howitzer and mount.

Walk behind tank; check condition of left track shoes and inside wedge nuts or lock pins and connectors.
Direct driver to move to rear; tighten inside cap screws as exposed.
Place tools in bag.

Drive tank forward at slow speed two tank lengths.

Drive tank to rear as directed by bog. Check the following:
Lubrication guide.

Cal .30 ammunition.
105-mm ammunition left of power tunnel.
Flare launcher and flares.
Submachine gun, ammunition, and personal equipment.

[1] The flame thrower, on tanks so equipped, is checked in this phase. The crew member using the weapon checks its condition, mechanism, and the fuel level in the tank in accordance with the appropriate published guide. It is mounted for use on order of the tank commander.

Tank Commander	Gunner	Bow Gunner	Driver	Cannoneer
	Clean chamber and breech mechanism.	Fold tarpaulin.	Submachine gun, ammunition, and personal equipment.	Periscope, spare, and spare heads. Safety belt. Turret exhaust fan.
	Check recoil oil. Lock howitzer traveling lock.			
Mount to rear deck. Check engine for leaks, vibrating accessories or parts.		Place tools on tarpaulin on rear deck. Mount to rear deck.		Connect break-away plugs.
Help bog close doors and stow tarpaulin. Pass tools to gunner. Take mounted post.	Receive and stow tools.	Close top engine doors. Stow tarpaulin. Open hatch. Take mounted post.	Ventilating blower. Connect break-away plugs.	

Check the follow-
ing:
Submachine gun,
ammunition,
and personal
equipment.
Periscope, spare,
spare heads,
and periscope
holder.
Spare vision
blocks.
Flag set.
Binoculars.
Mount antenna.
Make 1st echelon
radio check (par-
agraph 5 b).

Complete trip
ticket.

Lock turret
traversing
lock.
Connect break-
away plugs.

Check the fol-
lowing:
Gun book,
manuals,
and acci-
dent form.
Bow gun and
mount (ad-
just head-
space).
Cal .30 am-
munition.
Submachine
gun, am-
munition,
and per-
sonal
equip-
ment.

85

Tank Commander	Gunner	Bow Gunner	Driver	Cannoneer
		105-mm ammunition behind seat and in right sponson. Escape hatch. Periscopes, spare, and spare heads. Tripod mount. Hull drain valve. Hand fire extinguisher.		
Connect breakaway plugs.		Connect breakaway plugs.		

Command: REPORT (interphone check).

Report READY to platoon leader.

Report "Gunner ready".

Report "Bog ready".

Report "Driver ready".

Report "Loader ready".

40. DURING OPERATION INSPECTION, M4A3. This is a continuous process for all crew members.

Tank Commander	Gunner	Bow Gunner	Driver	Cannoneer
Remain alert to unusual noises or conditions. Check radio and interphone system. Check security of: Radio antenna. Outside fixtures and equipment.	Check operation of elevation and traversing mechanisms. Check security of: Turret lock. Howitzer.	Watch instruments. Listen for unusual noises. Check security of bow gun.	Check all instruments carefully. Check controls. Listen for unusual noises.	Check stowage of equipment in turret. Check security of: Coaxial gun. Radio. AA gun.

41. HALT INSPECTION, M4A3. The length of halt determines how much of the following inspection will be completed and the normal priority of operations. The tank commander will be informed of the length of halt and will indicate how much time is to be allotted to inspection and how much for relief of the crew members. (During the inspection, the turret is traversed as necessary to facilitate those operations requiring it.)

Tank Commander	Gunner	Bow Gunner	Driver	Cannoneer
Command: PERFORM HALT INSPECTION.				
Disconnect breakaway plugs.	Disconnect breakaway plugs.	Disconnect breakaway plugs.	Disconnect breakaway plugs.	Disconnect breakaway plugs.
Check radio for security.	Release turret lock.	Dismount.	Idle engine (run 2 minutes before stopping).	Turn on radio speaker.
Emerge from turret.	Elevate howitzer; check traverse.	Check under tank for fuel, oil or water leaks.	Check instruments.	Man AA gun.

88

Clean vision blocks, all turret periscopes, and telescope.	Check sight adjustment.	Mount to rear deck.	Dismount to rear deck.
Inspect tracks and tank suspension.	Check auxiliary generator operation.	Help driver open top doors.	Open top engine doors.
Supervise halt inspection.	Check coaxial gun and mount.	Check the following:	Check engine operation.
	Check smoke mortar.	Fuel level in all tanks.	Inspect engine compartment.
	Check air cleaners.	Engine coolant level.	Take mounted post.
	Check firing controls.	Outside equipment.	Stop engine (use fuel cut-off).
	Check howitzer and mount.	Engine oil level.[1]	Check the following:

[1] Engine oil level checked through rear door on earlier model engines, through top door on later models.

Tank Commander	Gunner	Bow Gunner	Driver	Cannoneer
	Place howitzer in traveling position.	Close doors. Dismount.	Steering levers. Gear shift lever. Parking brake.	
	Lock turret lock.	Open rear door; check oil level; close door.[1]	Clutch free travel. Transmission oil level and temperature.	
	Check stowage of equipment in turret. Connect breakaway plugs.	Help driver check lights.	Service and blackout lights.	
		Check final drives for	Driver's and bog's com-'	

Take mounted post.		leaks or ex-cessive tem-peratures.	partments for oil leaks.	Resume mounted post.
Connect breakaway plugs.		Check towing shackles.	Clean peri-scopes.	Turn off speaker.
Command: REPORT.		Take mounted post.	Connect break-away plugs.	Connect break-away plugs.
		Clean peri-scopes.		
		Connect break-away plugs.		
	Report "Gunner ready".	Report "Bog ready".	Report "Driver ready".	Report "Loader ready".

[1] Engine oil level checked through rear door on earlier model engines, through top door on later models.

91

42. AFTER OPERATION MAINTENANCE, M4A3. a. After operation the tank is immediately given whatever servicing and maintenance is needed to prepare it in every way for further sustained action. This servicing covers all the points listed in the Before Operation Inspection and covers them in the same order, with obvious modifications. (For example, the tank is locked at the end of the inspection instead of being unlocked at the beginning; the check for leaks under the tank is more effective after it has stood for awhile; battery switches are turned off rather than on and only after all checks requiring use of battery power; equipment is covered and stowed rather than being uncovered and made ready for use.)

b. The tank will be completely cleaned, serviced, and replenished (fuel, oil (all types), grease, coolant, ammunition (all types), first aid kit, water, and rations). *All special precautions against fire will be observed while refueling.* Crew members will perform the following additional operations not covered in the Before Operation Inspection.

Tank Commander	Gunner	Bow Gunner	Driver	Cannoneer
Command: PER-FORM AFTER OPERATION MAINTEN-ANCE.				
Complete trip ticket; forward to	Clean all weapons.		Idle engine 2 minutes be-	Help gunner clean

Tank Commander	Gunner	Bow Gunner	Driver	Cannoneer
platoon leader, together with report of any necessary 2d echelon maintenance, fuel, lubricants, ammunition and rations required.	Help driver clean tank. Help gunner clean weapons.	Help gunner clean weapons.	fore stopping, Clean tank suspension and outside of tank. Help gunner clean weapons.	weapons.

43. PERIODIC ADDITIONAL SERVICES, M4A3. Services performed weekly in garrison; in combat and on maneuvers they are performed after each field operation.

Tank Commander	Gunner	Bow Gunner	Driver	Cannoneer
Command: FALL IN; PREPARE FOR INSPECTION. Inspect crew. Command: PERFORM INSPECTION.	Stand inspection.	Stand inspection.	Stand inspection.	Stand inspection.

Tank Commander	Gunner	Bow Gunner	Driver	Cannoneer
Supervise inspection.	Mount to turret. Clean turret. Clean and touch up any rust spots in turret.	Mount to rear deck; help driver clean engine and engine compartment.	Open engine doors and clean engine and engine compartment. Take mounted post.	Mount to turret. Clean batteries and case. Test batteries with hydrometer. Bring cells to proper water level.
	Dismount.	Operate and check hull drain valves in engine compartment. Take mounted post.	Clean driver's compartment and left interior of hull.	Operate auxiliary generator to charge batteries. Dismount.

Clean bog's compartment and right interior of hull.

Operate and check hull drain valve.

Operate and check hull drain valve.

Drive tank forward as required for tightening wedge nuts.

Help gunner tighten wedge nuts and inspect track.

Perform 250-mile lubrication, referring to appropriate guide.

Close engine doors.

Help perform 250-mile lubrication.

Tighten all wedge nuts and inspect track.

Help perform 250-mile lubrication.

Help perform 250-mile lubrication.

Tank Commander	Gunner	Bow Gunner	Driver	Cannoneer
		Take mounted post; clean and touch up rust spots in bog's compartment.	Take mounted post; clean and touch up rust spots in driver's compartment.	
Command: REPORT.				
	Report "Gunner ready".			
		Report "Bog ready".		
			Report "Driver ready".	
				Report "Loader ready".

Section X

DESTRUCTION
OF EQUIPMENT

44. GENERAL. a. The destruction of materiel requires a command decision and will be undertaken only on authority delegated by division or higher commanders. Destruction is ordered only after every possible measure for the preservation or salvage of the materiel has been taken, and when in the judgment of the person exercising the authority such action is necessary to prevent.

(1) Its abandonment in the combat zone.

(2) Its capture intact by the enemy.

(3) Its use by the enemy, if captured, against our own or allied troops.

(4) Knowledge of its existence, functioning, or exact specifications from reaching enemy intelligence.

b. The principles to be followed are—

(1) Methods for the destruction of materiel subject to capture or abandonment in the combat zone must be adequate, uniform, and easily followed in the field.

(2) Destruction must be as complete as available time, equipment, and personnel will permit. If thorough destruction of all parts cannot be completed, the most important features of the materiel should be destroyed, and parts essential to the operation or use of the materiel which cannot be easily duplicated, should be ruined or destroyed. The same essential parts must be destroyed on all like units to

prevent the enemy from constructing one complete unit from several damaged ones 'by "cannibalism".

c. Crews will be trained in the prescribed methods of destruction, but training will not involve the actual destruction of materiel.

d. (1) The methods outlined in the paragraphs below are given in order of effectiveness. If method No. 1 cannot be used, destruction should be accomplished by one of the other methods in order of priority shown. Adhere to the sequences.

(2) Certain methods require special tools and equipment, such as TNT and incendiary grenades, which normally may not be items of issue. The issue of such special tools and material, the vehicles for which issued, and the conditions under which destruction will be effected are command decisions in each case, according to the tactical situation.

45. DESTRUCTION OF HOWITZER. Remove sights. If evacuation is possible, carry the sights; if evacuation is not possible, thoroughly smash all periscopic sights and the telescope.

a. Method No. 1. (1) Open drain plugs on recoil mechanism, allowing recoil fluid to drain. *It is not necessary to wait for the recoil fluid to drain completely before firing the howitzer as in (4) below.*

(2) Place an *armed (safety pin removed)* antitank grenade, HE, or *armed (safety pin removed)* antitank rocket in the tube about 6 inches in front of, and with the ogive nose end toward, the HE shell in (3) below.

(3) Set fuze on an HE shell at "superquick", insert shell in the piece and close the breech.

(4) Attach a piece of string to the howitzer firing linkage in such a way that it may be fired by pulling

the string. Dismount from the tank (down to the left rear) and fire the piece. Elapsed time: Approximately 2 to 3 minutes.

b. Method No. 2. Insert from three to five ½-pound TNT blocks in the bore near the muzzle, eight to ten in the chamber. Close the breechblock as far as possible without damaging the safety fuze. Plug the muzzle tightly with earth to a distance of approximately 11 inches from the muzzle. Detonate the TNT charges simultaneously.

c. Method No. 3. With another gun, fire HE, HEAT or AP projectiles at the tube of the piece until it is rendered useless.

d. Method No. 4. Insert four unfuzed M14 incendiary grenades, end to end, midway in the tube at 0° elevation. Ignite these four grenades with a fifth equipped with a 15-second Bickford fuze. The metal from the grenades will fuse with the tube and fill the grooves. Elapsed time: 2 to 3 minutes.

46. DESTRUCTION OF MACHINE GUNS. a. Method No. 1. (1) *Caliber .30 machine gun.* Field strip. Use barrel as a sledge. Raise cover until vertical; smash cover down toward front. Deform and break backplate; deform T-slot. Wedge lock frame, back down, into top of casing between top plate and extractor cam; place chamber end of barrel over lock frame depressors and break off depressors. Insert barrel extension into back of casing, allowing the shank to protrude; knock off shank by striking with barrel from the side. Deform and crack casing by striking with barrel at side plate corners nearest feedway. Elapsed time: 2½ minutes.

(2) *Caliber .50 machine gun.* Field strip. Use barrel as a sledge. Raise cover; lay bolt in feedway; lower

cover on bolt; smash cover down over bolt. Deform backplate. Wedge buffer into rear of casing allowing depressors to protrude; break off depressors by striking with barrel. Lay barrel extension on its side. Hold down with one foot, break off the shank. Deform casing by striking side plates just back of the feedway. Elapsed time: 3½ minutes.

b. Method No. 2. Insert bullet point of complete round into muzzle and bend case slightly, distending mouth of case to permit pulling of bullet. Spill powder from case, retaining sufficient powder to cover the bottom of case to a depth of approximately ⅛ inch. Re-insert pulled bullet, point first, into the case mouth. Chamber and fire this round with the reduced charge; the bullet will stick in the bore. Chamber one complete round, lay weapon on ground, and fire with a 30-foot lanyard. Use the best available cover, as this means of destruction may be dangerous to the person destroying the weapon. Elapsed time: 2 to 3 minutes.

c. Small arms. Small arms cannot be adequately destroyed by firing with the bore stuck in the ground, with or without a bullet jammed in the muzzle.

d. Machine gun tripod mount, caliber .30 M2. Use machine gun barrel as a sledge. Deform traversing dial. Fold rear legs, turn mount over on head, stand on folded rear legs, knock off traversing dial locking screw, pintle lock, and deform head assembly. Deform folded rear legs so as to prevent unfolding. Extend elevating screw and bend screw by striking with barrel; bend pintle yoke. Elapsed time: 2 minutes.

47. DESTRUCTION OF TANK. a. Method No. 1. (1) Remove and empty the portable fire extinguishers.

Smash the radio (paragraph 52). Puncture fuel tanks. Use fire of caliber .50 machine gun, or a cannon, or use a fragmentation grenade for this purpose. Place TNT charges as follows: 3 pounds between engine oil cooler and right fuel tank; 2 pounds under left side of transmission as far forward as possible. Insert tetryl nonelectric caps with at least 5 feet of safety fuse in each charge. Ignite the fuses and take cover. Elapsed time: 1 to 2 minutes, if charges are prepared beforehand and carried in the vehicle.

(2) If sufficient time and materials are available, additional destruction of track-laying vehicles may be accomplished by placing a 2-pound TNT charge about the center of each track-laying assembly. Detonate those charges in the same manner as the others.

(3) If charges are prepared beforehand and carried in the vehicle, keep the caps and fuses separated from the charges until used.

b. **Method No. 2.** Remove and empty the portable fire extinguishers. Smash the radio (paragraph 52). Puncture fuel tanks (see *a* (1) above). Fire on the vehicle using adjacent tanks, antitank or other artillery, or antitank rockets or grenades. Aim at engine, suspension, and armament in the order named. If a good fire is started, the vehicle may be considered destroyed. Elapsed time: About 5 minutes per vehicle. Destroy the last remaining vehicle by the best means available.

48. DESTRUCTION OF AMMUNITION. a. General.
(1) Time will not usually permit the destruction of all ammunition in forward combat zones.

(2) When sufficient time and materials are available, ammunition may be destroyed as indicated

below. At least 30 to 60 minutes may be required to destroy adequately the ammunition carried by combat units.

(3) In general, the methods and safety precautions outlined in Chapter 4, TM 9–1900, should be followed whenever possible.

b. Unpacked complete round ammunition. (1) Stack ammunition in small piles. (Small arms ammunition may be heaped.) Stack or pile most of the available gasoline in cans and drums around the ammunition. Place on pile all available inflammable material such as rags, scrap wood, and brush. Pour the remaining available gasoline over the pile. Sufficient inflammable material must be used to insure a very hot fire. Ignite the gasoline and take cover.

(2) Destroy 105-mm ammunition by sympathetic detonation, using TNT. Stack the ammunition in two stacks about 3 inches apart, with fuses in each stack toward each other. Place TNT charges between the stacks. Use 1 pound of TNT per four or five rounds of ammunition. Detonate all charges of TNT simultaneously from cover.

c. Packed complete round ammunition. (1) Stack the boxed or bundled ammunition in small piles. Cover with all available inflammable materials, such as rags, scrap wood, brush, and gasoline in drums or cans. Pour gasoline over the pile. Ignite the gasoline and take cover. (Small arms ammunition must be broken out of the boxes or cartons before burning.)

(2) (a) The destruction of packed complete round ammunition by sympathetic detonation with TNT is not advocated for use in forward combat zones. To insure satisfactory destruction involves putting TNT in alternate cases or bundles of ammunition, a time-consuming job.

(*b*) In rear areas or fixed installations, sympathetic detonation may be used to destroy large ammunition supplies if destruction by burning is not feasible. Stack the boxes, placing in alternate boxes in each row sufficient TNT blocks to insure the use of 1 pound of TNT per four to five rounds of 105-mm ammunition. Place the TNT blocks at the fuse end of the rounds. Detonate all TNT charges simultaneously. See FM 5–25 for details of demolition planning and procedure.

d. Miscellaneous. Grenades, antitank mines, and antitank rockets may be destroyed by the methods outlined in **b** and **c** above for complete rounds. The amount of TNT necessary to detonate these munitions is considered less than that required for detonating artillery shells. Fuses, boosters, detonators, and similar material should be destroyed by burning.

49. FIRE CONTROL EQUIPMENT. Fire control equipment, including optical sights and binoculars, is difficult to replace. It should be the last equipment to be destroyed. If evacuation of personnel is made, all possible items of fire control equipment should be carried. If evacuation of personnel is not possible, fire control equipment must be thoroughly destroyed as indicated below.

a. Firing tables, trajectory charts, slide rules and similar items should be thoroughly burned.

b. All optical equipment that cannot be evacuated will be thoroughly smashed.

50. RADIO EQUIPMENT. a. Books and papers. Instruction books, circuit and wiring diagrams, records of all kinds for radio equipment, code books, and registered documents will be destroyed by burning.

b. Radio sets. (1) Shear off all panel knobs, dials, etc., with an ax. Break open the set compartment by smashing in the panel face, then knock off the top, bottom, and sides. The object is to destroy the panel and expose the chassis. On top of the chassis, strike all tubes and circuit elements with the ax head. On the under side of the chassis, if it can be reached, use the ax to shear or tear off wires and small circuit units. Break sockets and cut unit and circuit wires. Smash or cut tubes, coils, crystal holders, microphones, earphones, and batteries. Break mast sections and break mast base at the insulator.

(2) When possible, pile up smashed equipment, pour on gas or oil, nad set it on fire. If other inflammable material, such as wood, is available, use it to increase the fire. Bury smashed parts.

INDEX

Knox 11-H-10-6-44-141C

Made in the USA
Charleston, SC
30 November 2011